Exploring Cho[rds]

The FJH Young Beginner Guitar [Method] 2

Philip Groeber
David Hoge
Leo Welch
Rey Sanchez

Contents

Production: Frank and Gail Hackinson
Production Coordinator: Philip Groeber
Special Editing: John and B.J. Sutherland, Carol Matz, Romana Hartmetz
Cover Design/Illustrations: Terpstra Design, San Francisco,
David B. Martin
Photography: Lynn Ivory, Master Photographer, Tallahassee
Cover Photo: courtesy of C.F. Martin Guitar & Co., Inc., Nazareth, PA
Engraving: Tempo Music Press, Inc.
Printer: Tempo Music Press, Inc.

ISBN-13: 978-1-56939-217-1

Review of Book 1

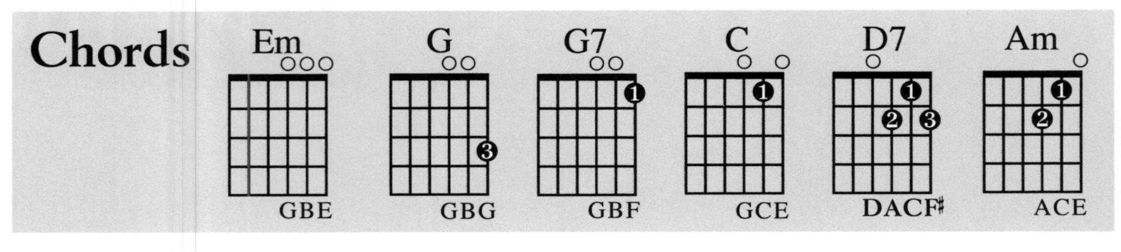

The student strums chords softly and evenly.
The teacher plays the melody throughout this book.

Strum Marks

- / = one beat
- 𝅗𝅥 = two beats
- 𝅗𝅥. = three beats
- 𝅝 = four beats
- 𝄽 = rest for one beat

She'll Be Comin' 'Round the Mountain

Traditional

Common Fingers and Guide Fingers

Common fingers are fingers that remain in position when changing between chords.

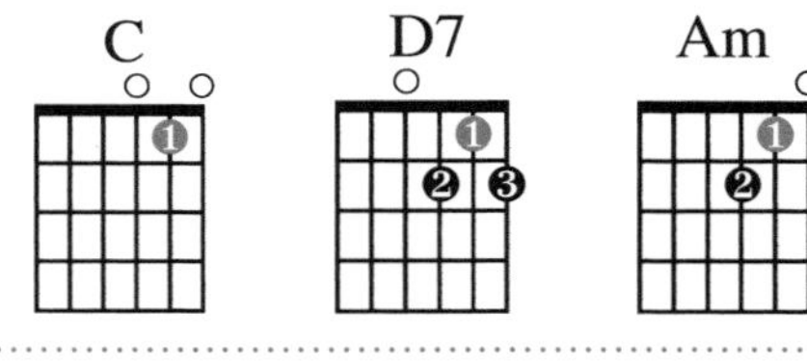

Guide fingers are fingers that keep gentle contact with the string when changing between chords.

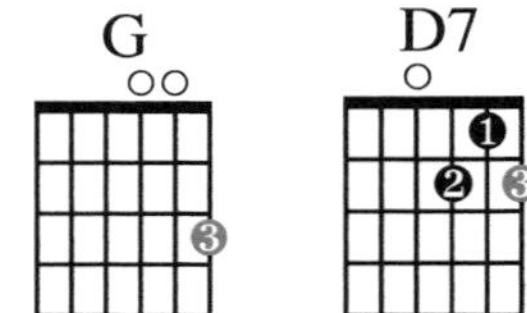

Molly Malone

Traditional Irish Melody

You are now ready to learn complete chords!

Complete Chords

THE E MINOR CHORD (Em)

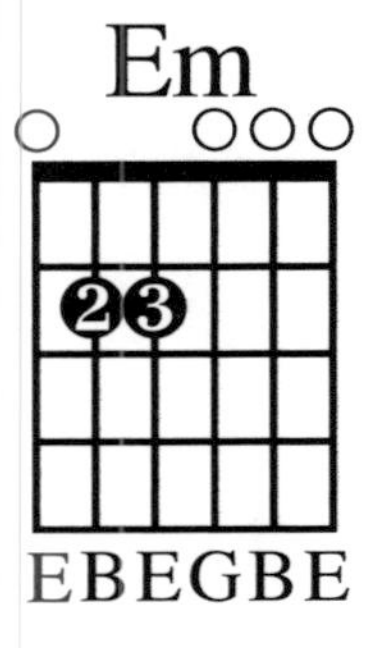

THE E MAJOR CHORD (E)

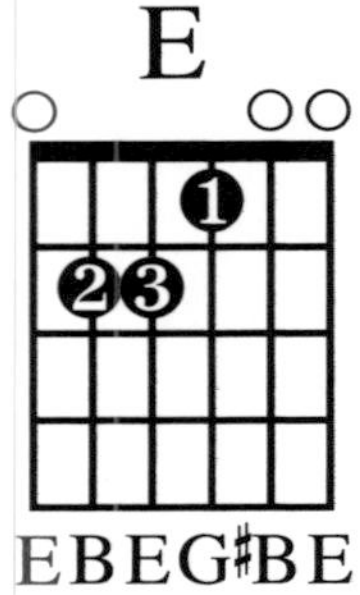

Strum all six strings for each chord.

Mostly Sunny

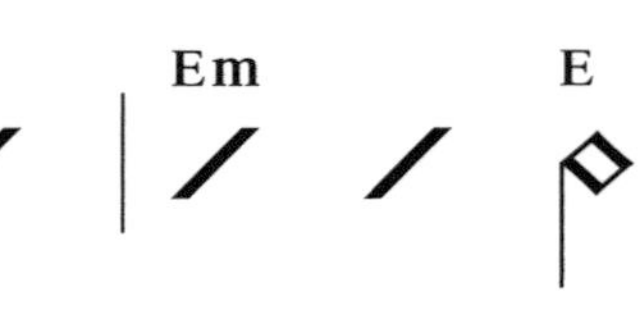

Although the E and the Em chords use all six strings, each of these chords is made up of three *different* notes: E major = E G♯ B; E minor = E G B.
Every chord has a **root**. The root is the letter name of the chord.
The lowest-pitched root of all new chords will be shown in color.

THE A SEVEN CHORD (A7)

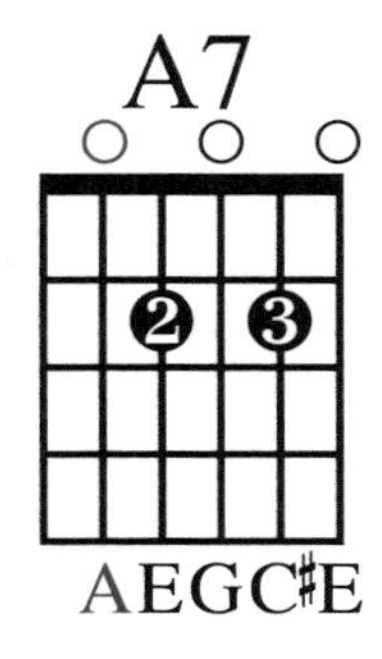

- Strum five strings when playing the A7 chord, as shown on the fingerboard chart.
- Notice that the Em and A7 chords have a similar left-hand shape.

Changing Your Ways

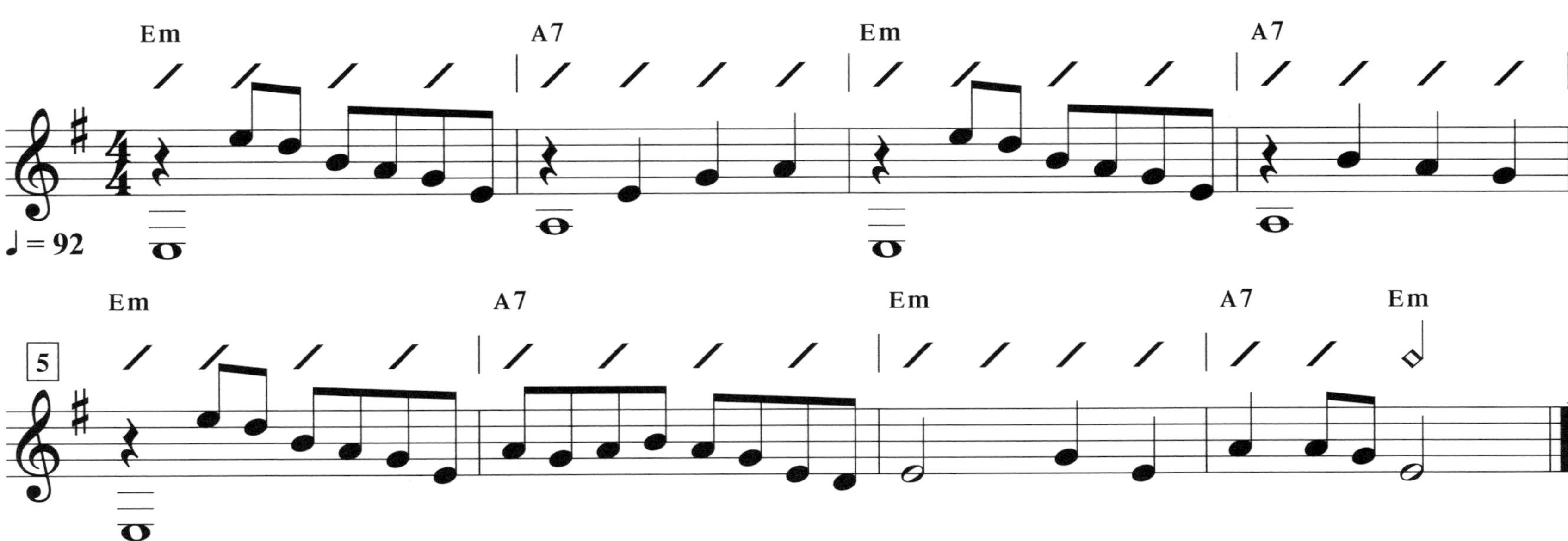

The A7 chord is made up of four different notes: A C♯ E G. The root is A.
You are now ready to learn the Root Strum technique on page six.

ROOT STRUM TECHNIQUE

The **Root Strum** is a very popular technique that makes it sound as if two people are playing at the same time!

- When playing in 4/4 time, use a downstroke to play the lowest-pitched root note (**R**) of the chord on beat one.
- Strum strings ③ ② ① on beats two, three and four.

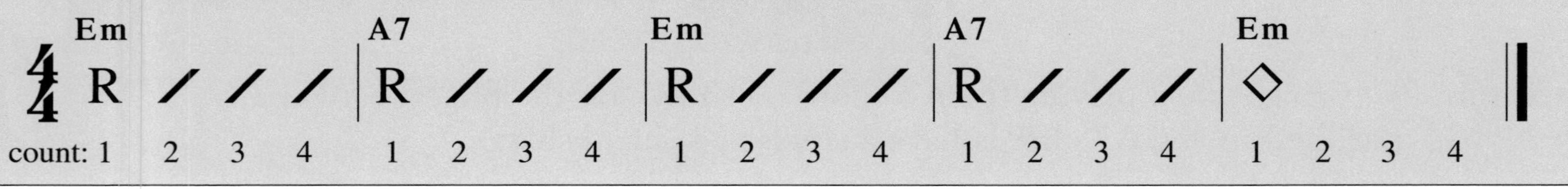

- When playing in 3/4 time, use a downstroke to play the lowest-pitched root note (**R**) of the chord on beat one.
- Strum strings ③ ② ① on beats two and three.

Em A7 Em A7 Em
R / / R / / R / / R / /
count: 1 2 3 1 2 3 1 2 3 1 2 3 1 2 3

The root note (**R**) should continue to sound as you strum the rest of the chord.

Play *Changing Your Ways* (page five) with the **Root Strum** technique as shown in the example.

Note to the teacher: Omit all of the whole notes when student is playing the Root Strum technique.

THE A MINOR CHORD (Am)

Lullaby
(*Aija, Anzit, Aija*)
Latvian Folk Song

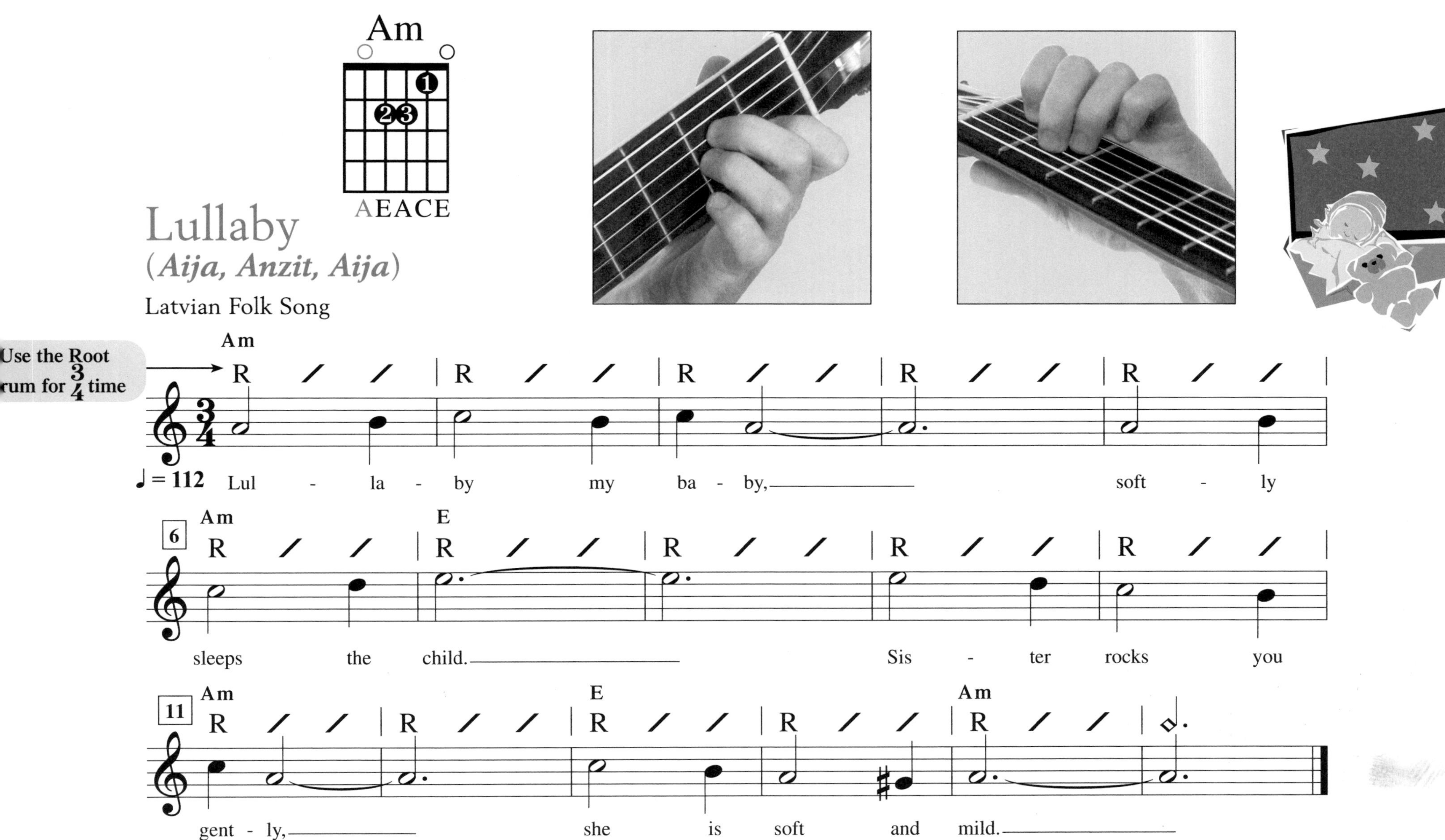

TECHNIQUE TIP

When using the Root Strum between Am and E, you may first play the open string root note, and then move your left-hand fingers to the new chord position.

THE G MAJOR CHORD (G)

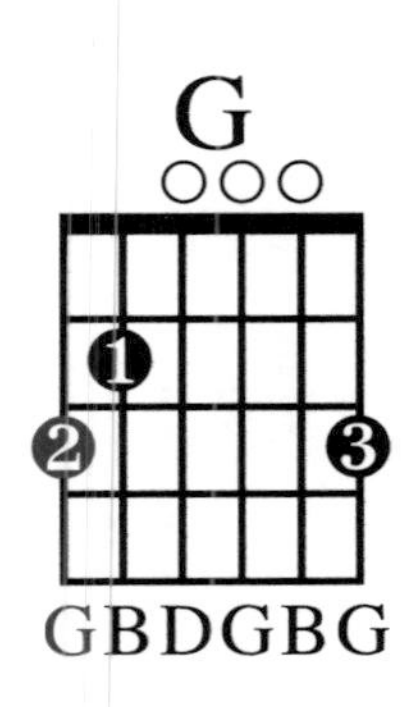

Merrily We Roll Along

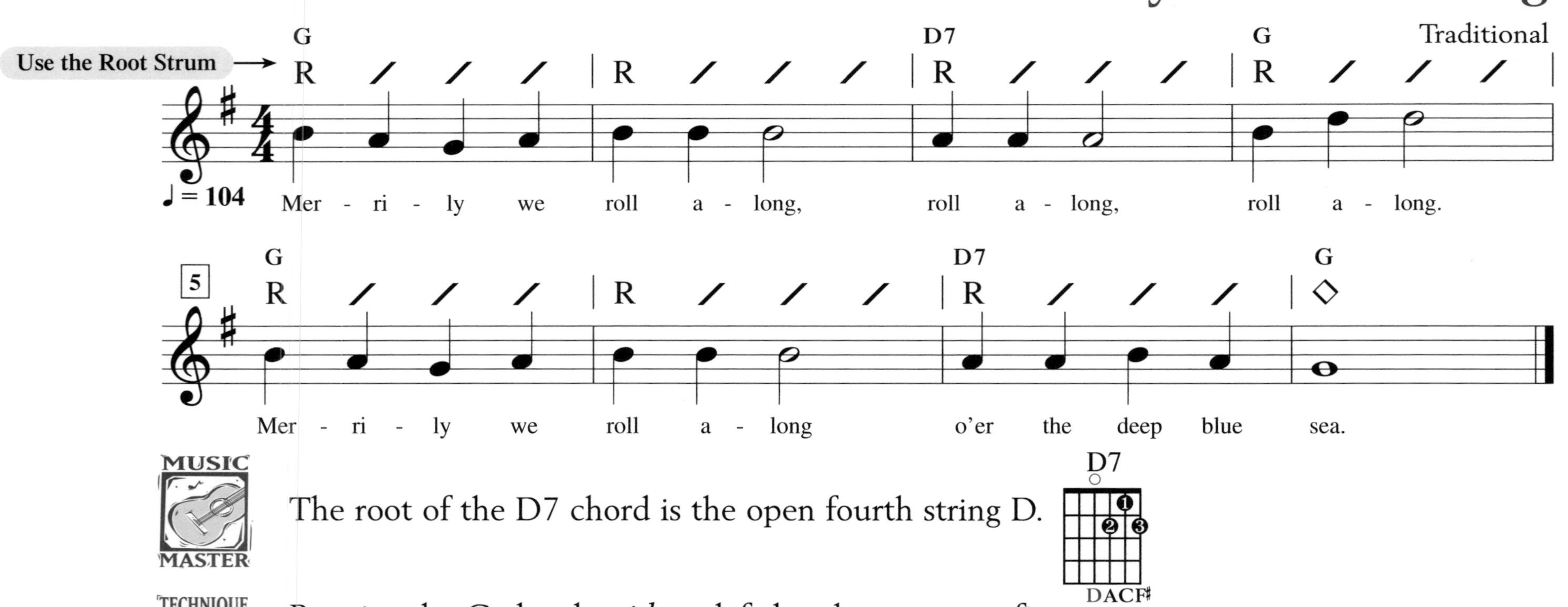

The root of the D7 chord is the open fourth string D.

Practice the G chords *without* left-hand pressure at first.
Then keep the correct hand position as you press the strings down.
Remember to use guide fingers whenever possible.

Stewball

American Folk Song

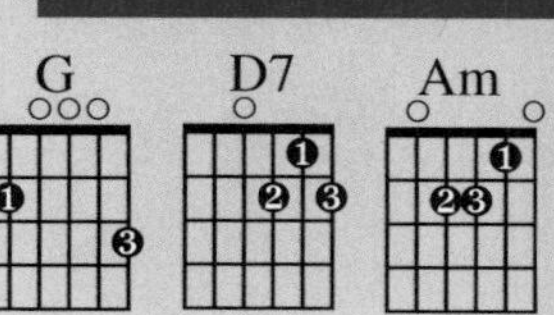

When the strum pattern is not indicated throughout the entire song, continue strumming in the same way.
The right hand not only strums the chords, but keeps an even beat, much like a drummer in a band.

When changing to a G chord using the Root Strum, you may place the root note (second finger ❷) down first.
After you play the root, place the rest of the chord.

THE C MAJOR CHORD (C)

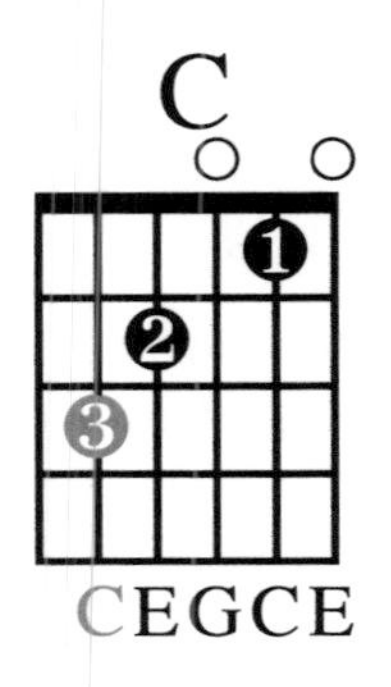

Treasure Chest

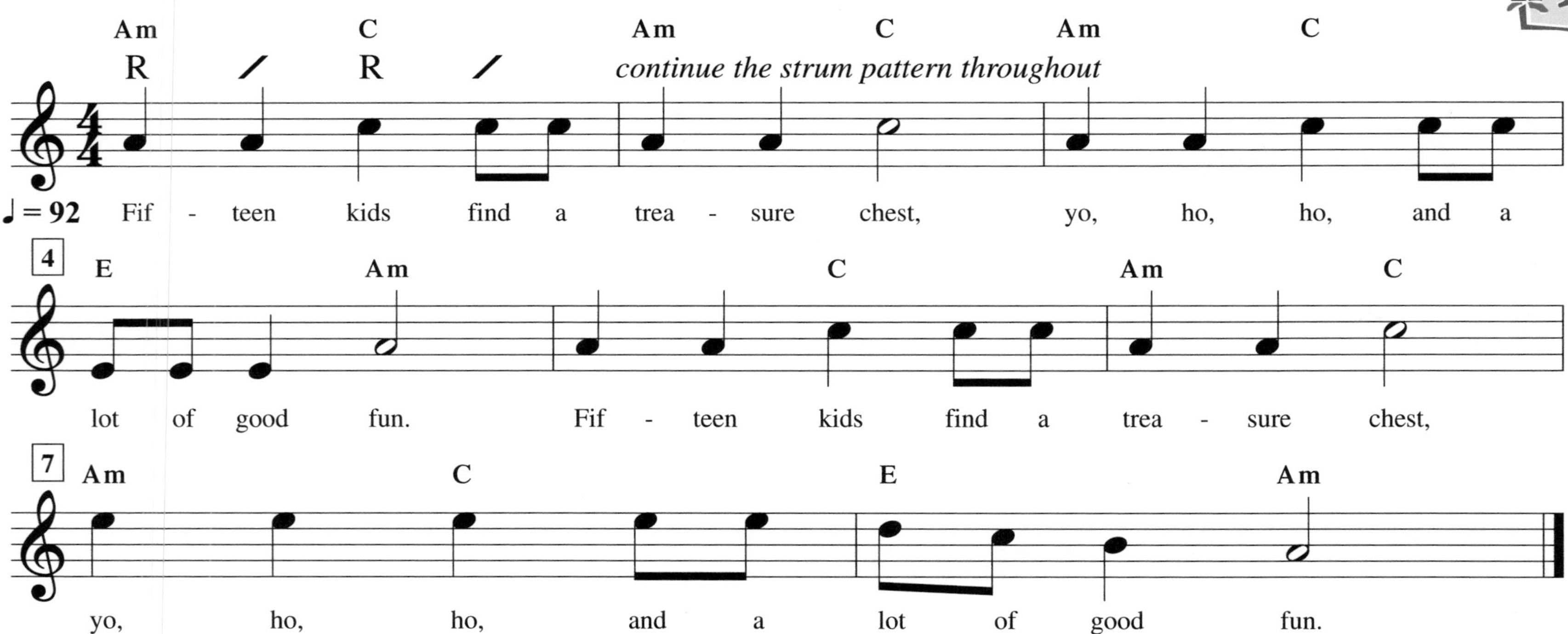

- *Treasure Chest* uses two chords in each measure.
  Notice the new Root Strum pattern (R / R /).
- Use a whole or half note strum to end a song when no strum is indicated.
- When changing between the Am and C chords, use two common fingers.

Am C

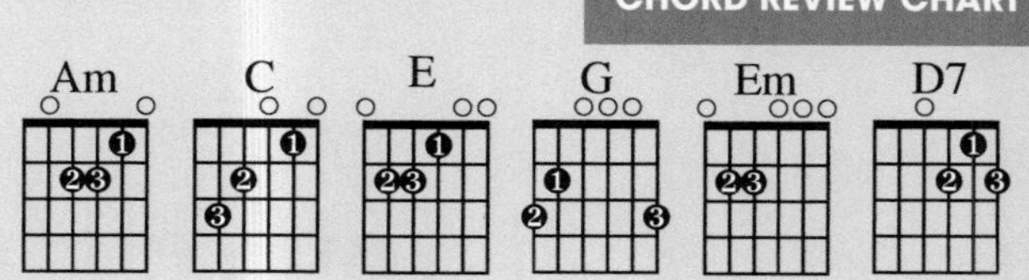

Strumming on the 1645

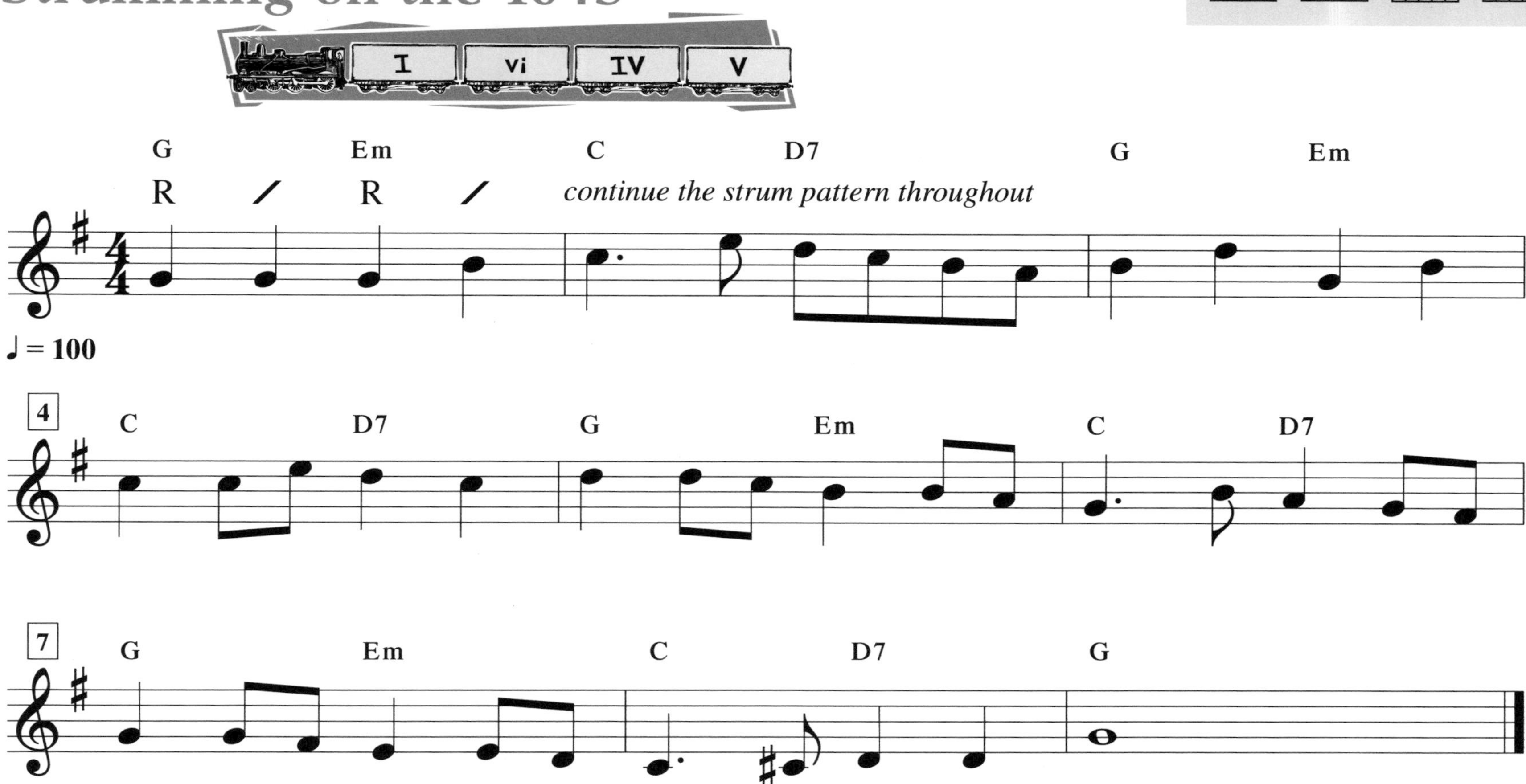

POWER PLAY

Ear Training

- Your teacher will play either an E chord or an Em chord.
- Using your ears only (no looking), identify the chord that you hear.
- Try this exercise with other chords as well.

Note to teacher: You may want to introduce an alternate fingering for Em at this time.

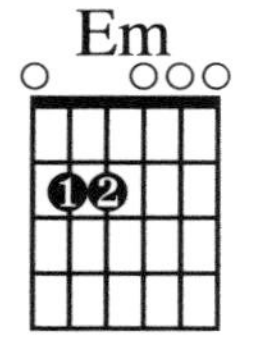

If You're Happy and You Know It

Traditional

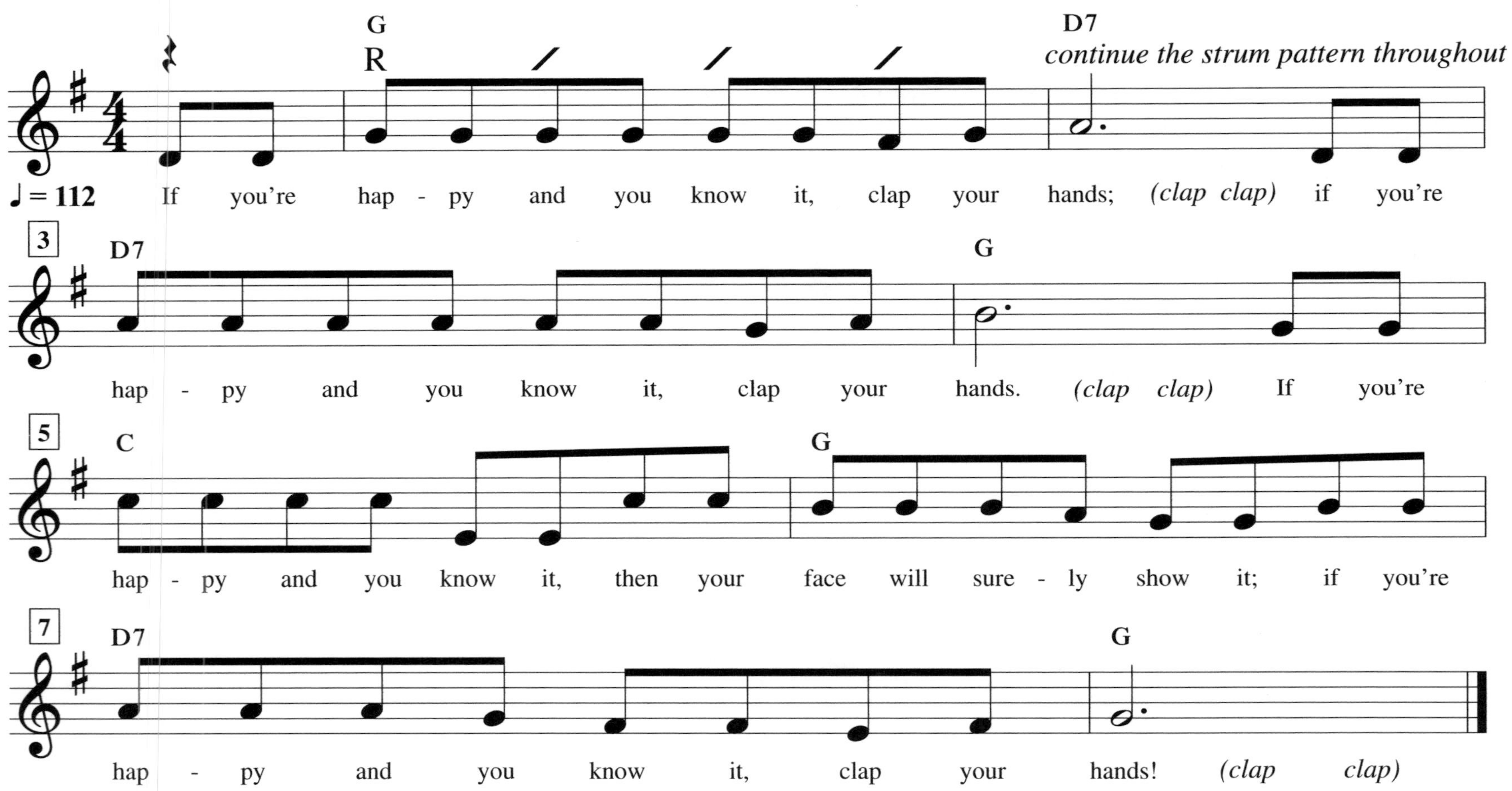

Practice changing smoothly between the G and C chords. Always look ahead to the next chord.

In measures 2, 4, and 8, strum the chords only on the handclaps (as shown in the example).

Folias de España

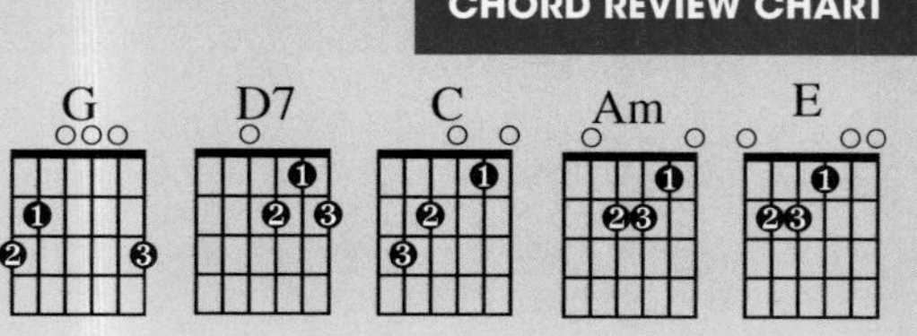

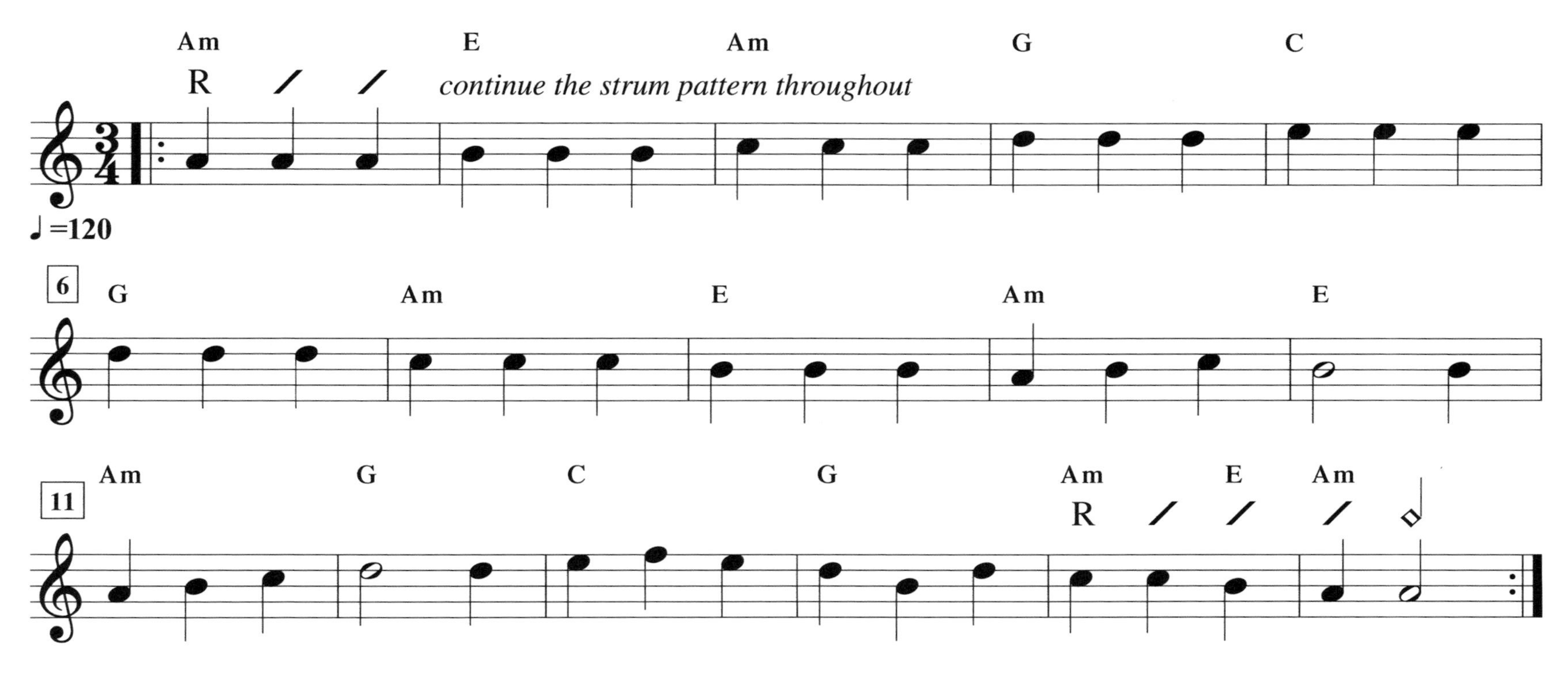

Music that is enclosed by repeat signs is to be played again.

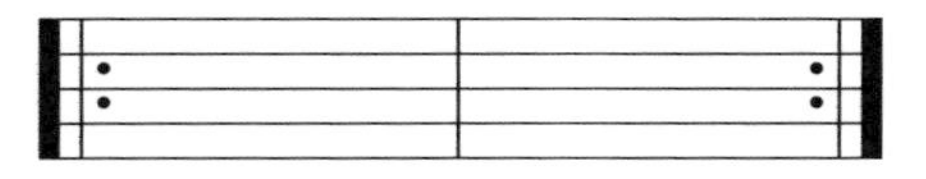

When practicing changing between two chords, give each finger a chance to be "first."

- If you tend to place your first finger down first, try placing your fingers in reverse order (❸ ❷ ❶). Try various other patterns (such as ❷ ❶ ❸, etc.).
- You may save energy by using no left-hand pressure while doing this exercise.

THE G SEVEN CHORD (G7)

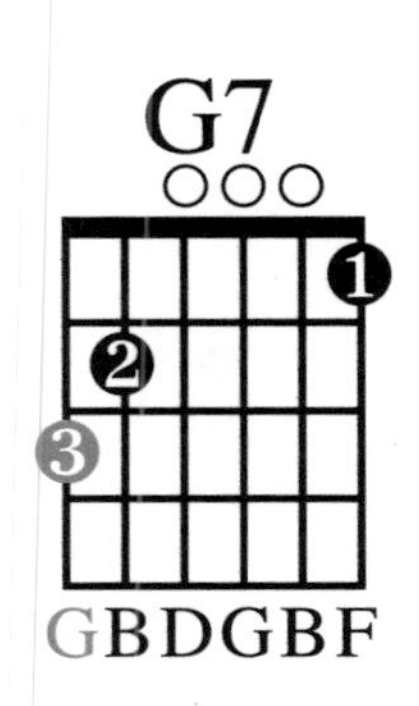

It Ain't Gonna Rain No More

Traditional

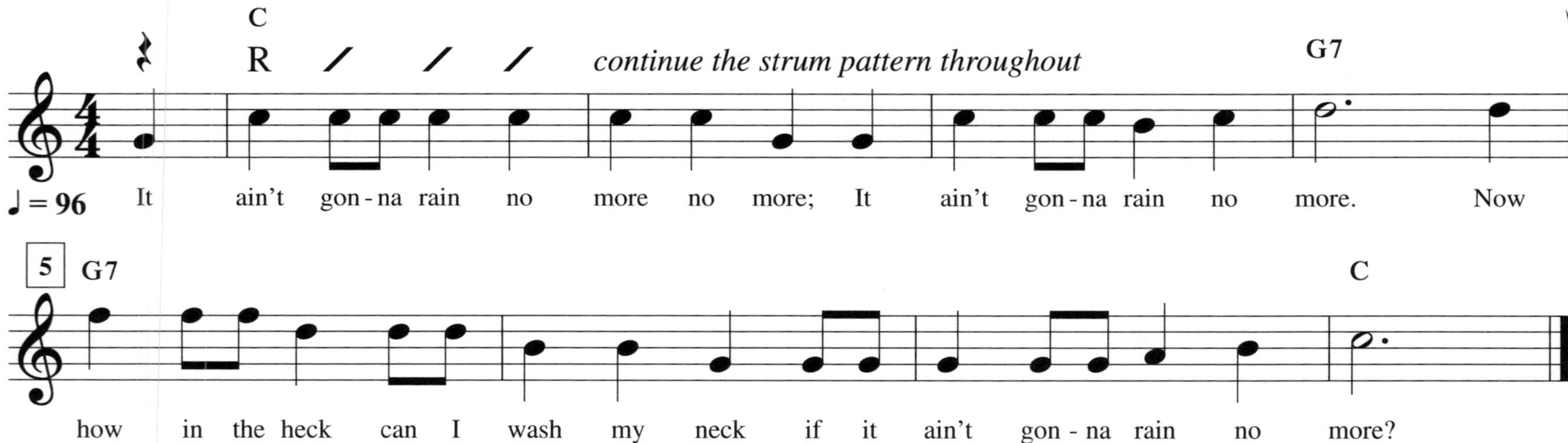

You now know how to play the complete versions of all chords learned in *Exploring Chords, Book 1*. Play your favorite songs from Book 1 using the complete chords that you have learned.

Notice that the C and G7 chords have similar shapes.
Use as little left-hand movement as possible when changing chords.

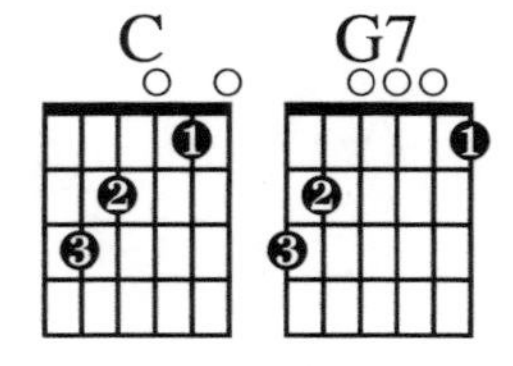

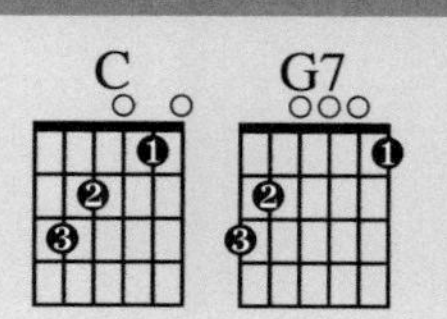

She Played Her Guitar

Early American Melody

Many songs begin with pick-up notes.
Do not begin strumming until the first chord name appears.

When playing the Root Strum, remember that you may place
(and play) the root note first, followed by the rest of the chord.

THE D MAJOR CHORD (D)

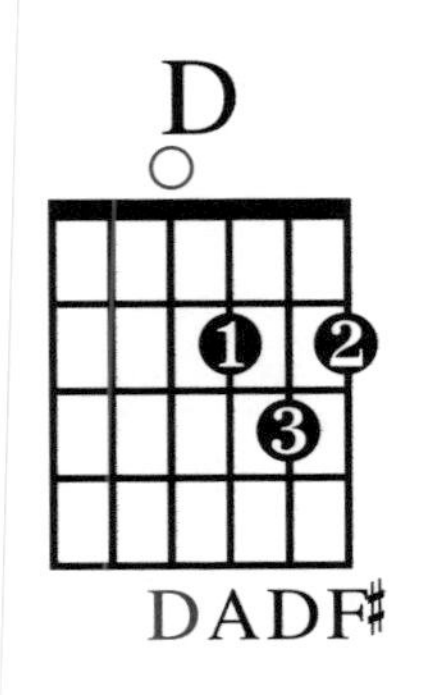

Oh Where, Oh Where Has My Little Dog Gone?

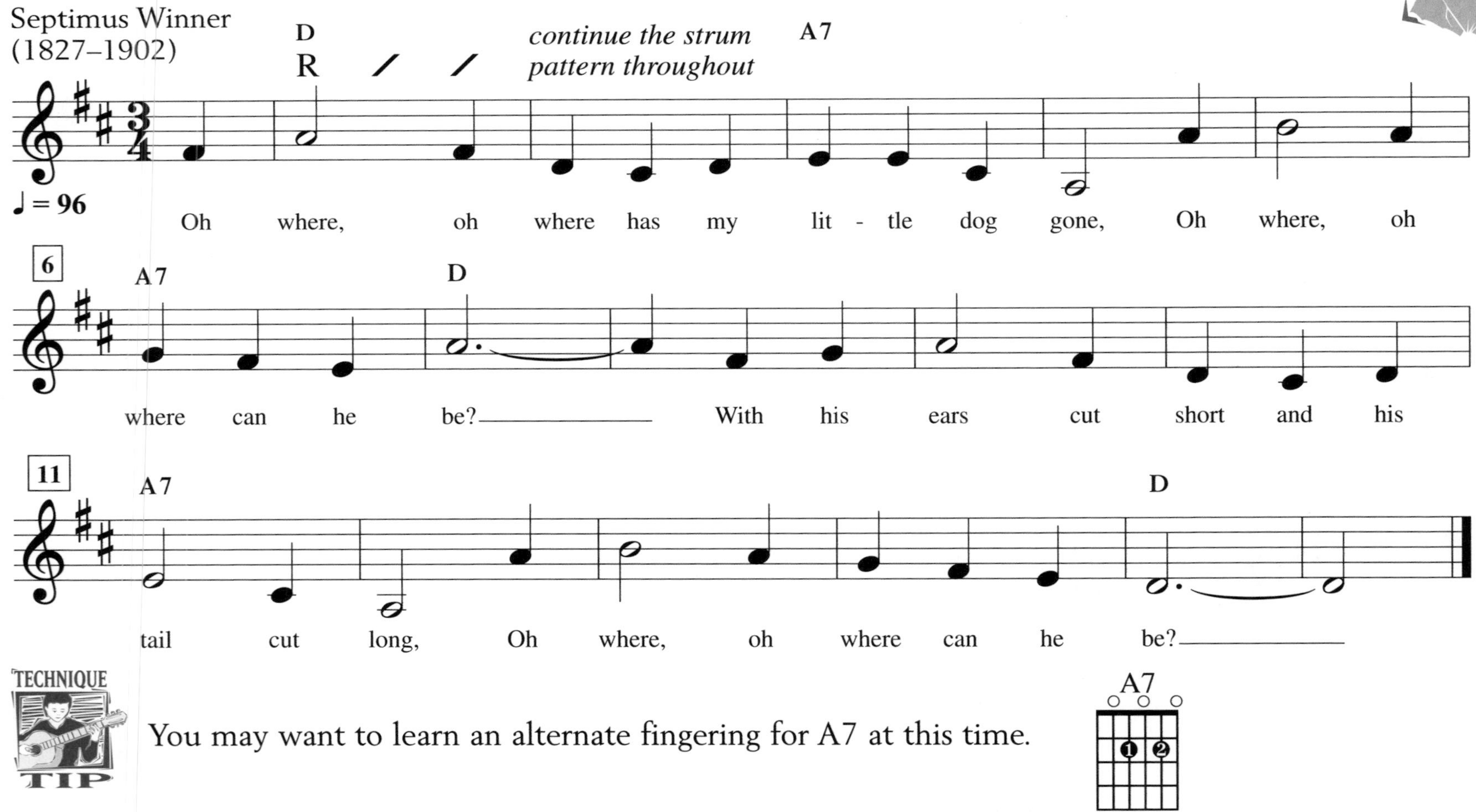

TECHNIQUE TIP

You may want to learn an alternate fingering for A7 at this time.

CHORD REVIEW CHART

D A7 G

When the Saints Go Marching In

Traditional American Folk Song

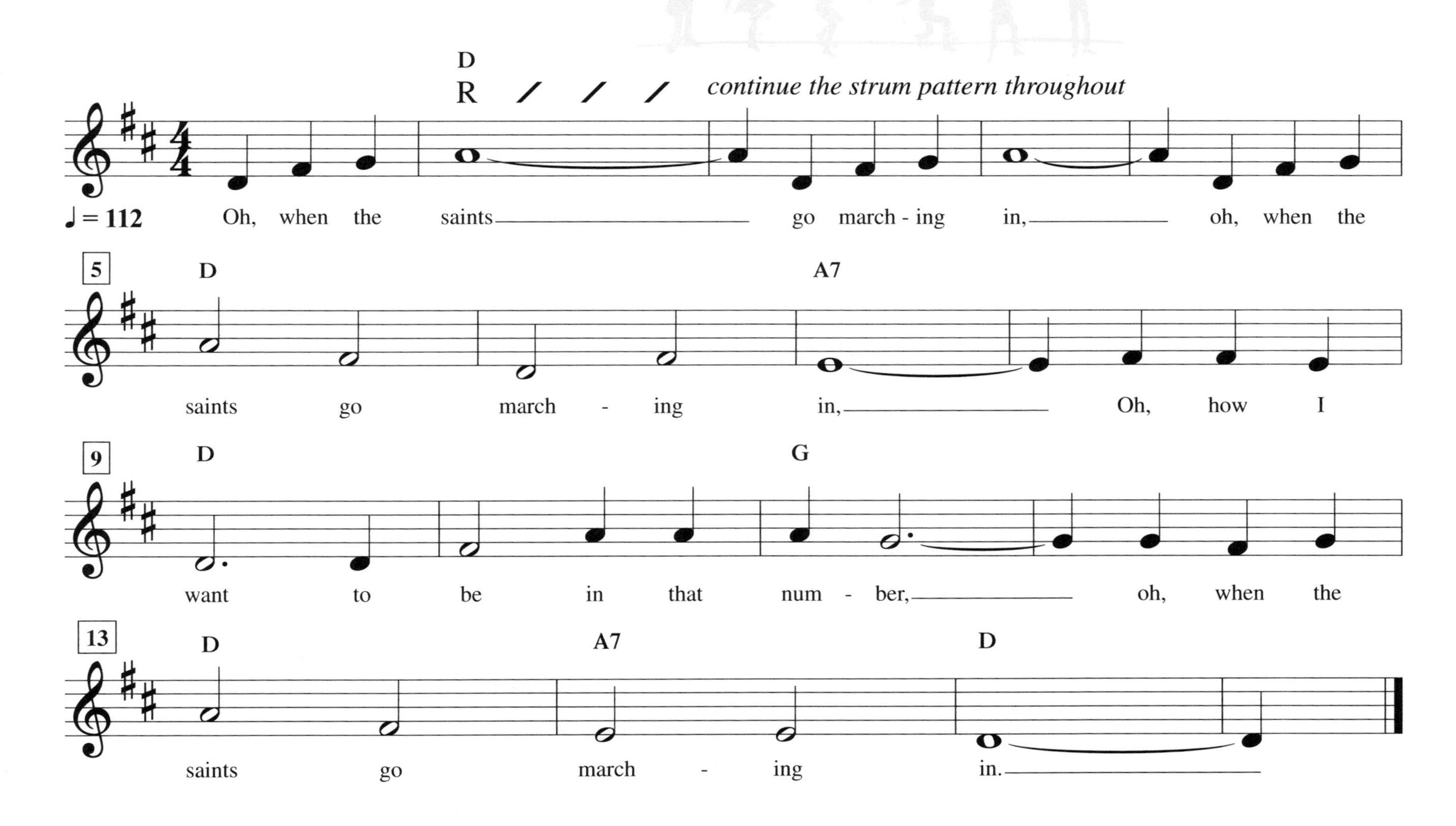

Chord Playing Goals:

- Memorize the chords you have learned so far.
- Strum the chords without pausing between chord changes.

THE B SEVEN CHORD (B7)

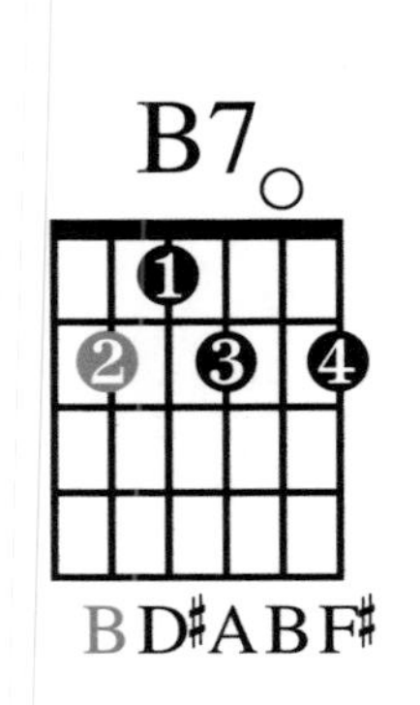

Romanza

Traditional Spanish Melody

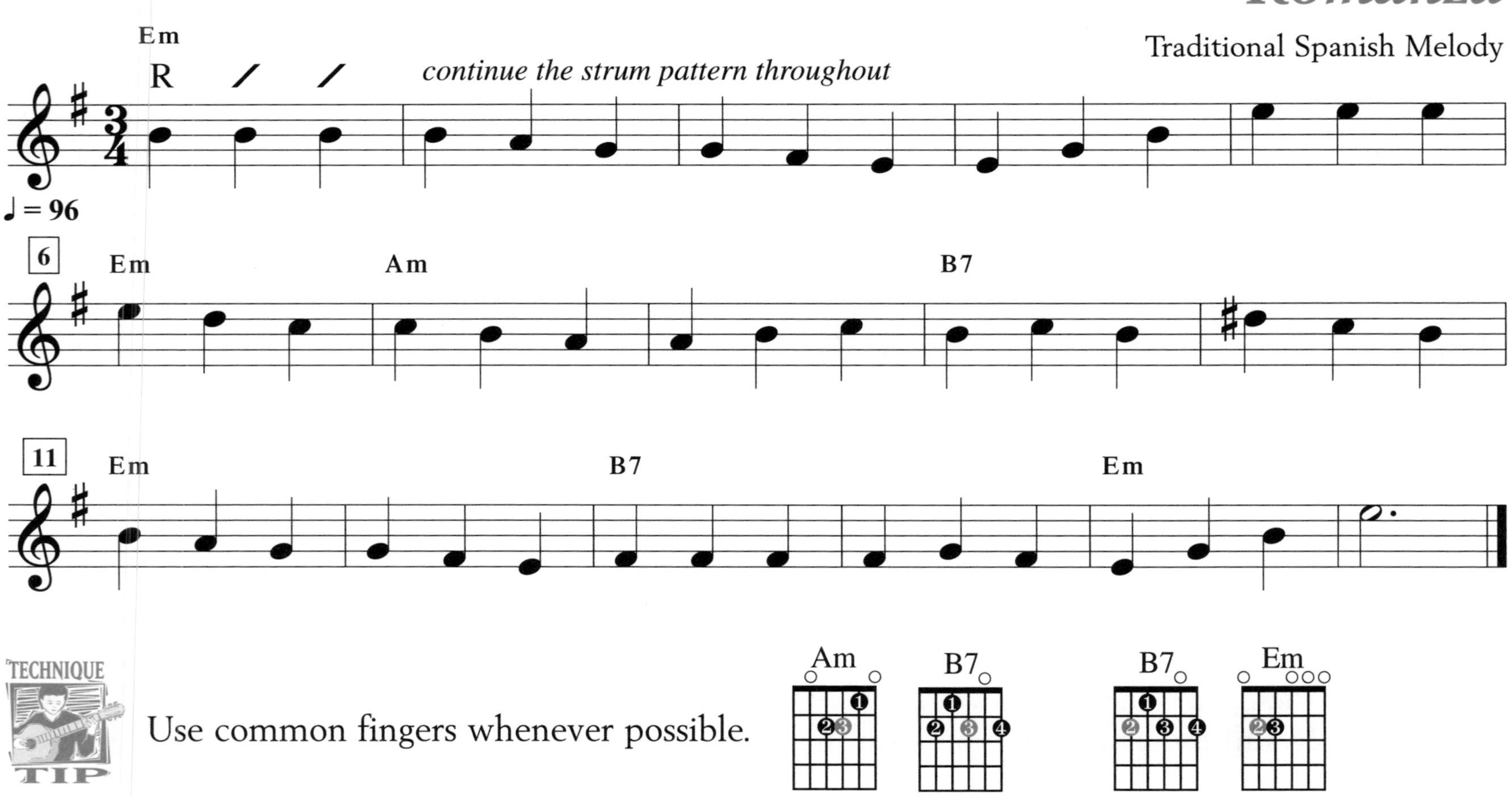

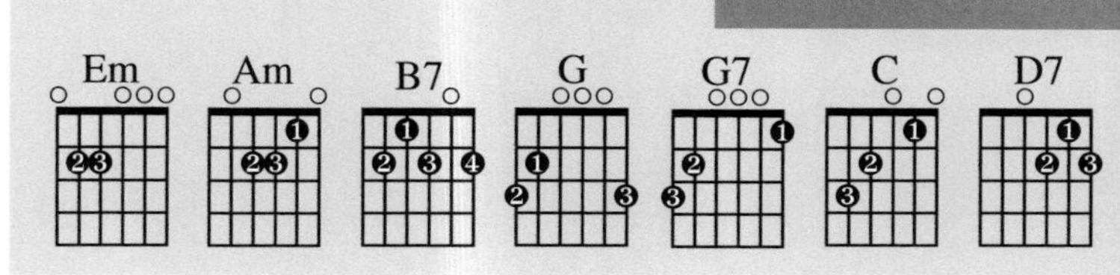

This Little Light of Mine

African-American Spiritual

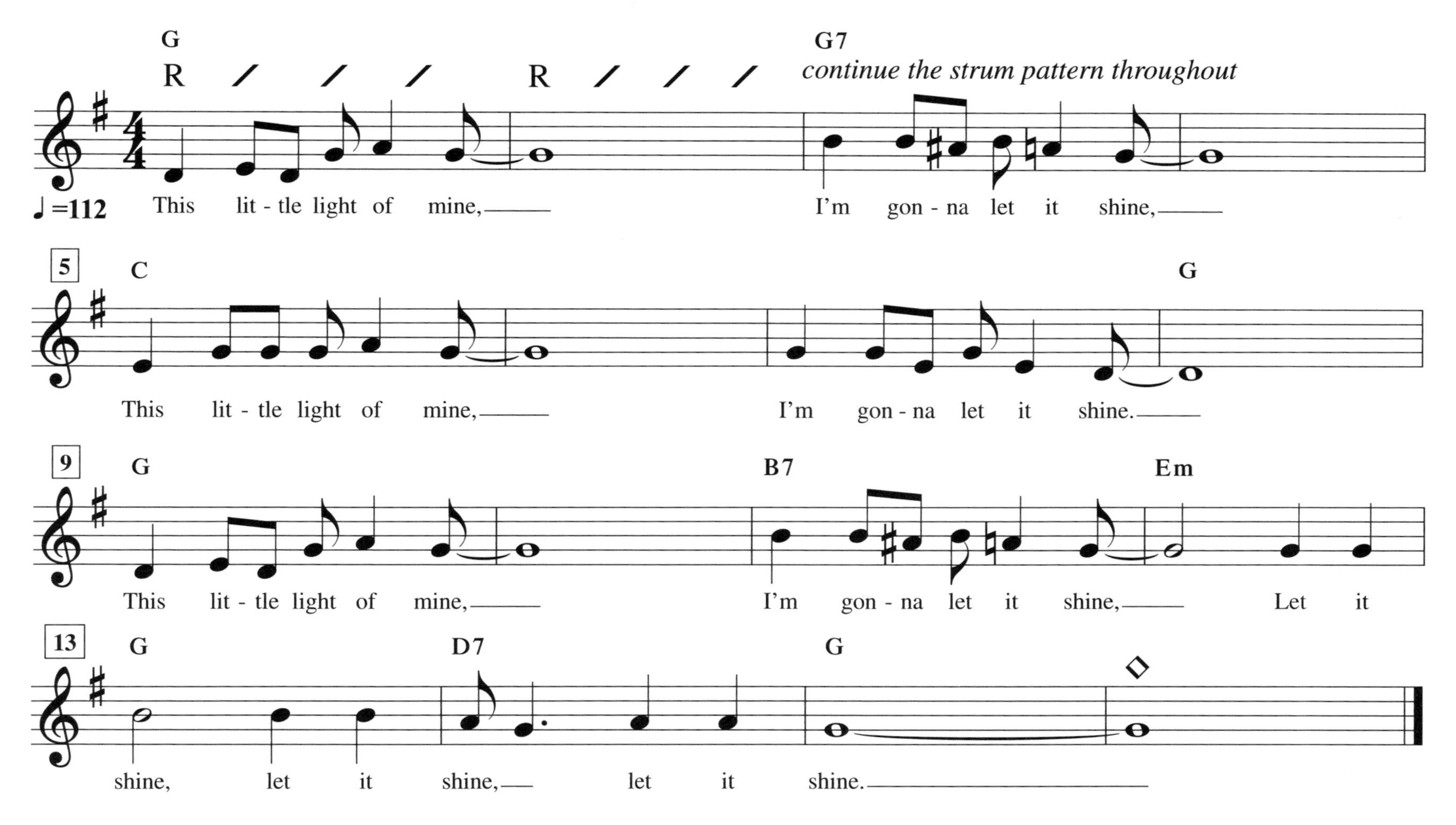

Ear Training

- Your teacher will play either a G chord or a G7 chord.
- Using your ears only (no looking), identify which chord you hear.
- Try this exercise with other chords as well, listening for the differences between major, minor, and seventh chords.

THE A MAJOR CHORD (A)

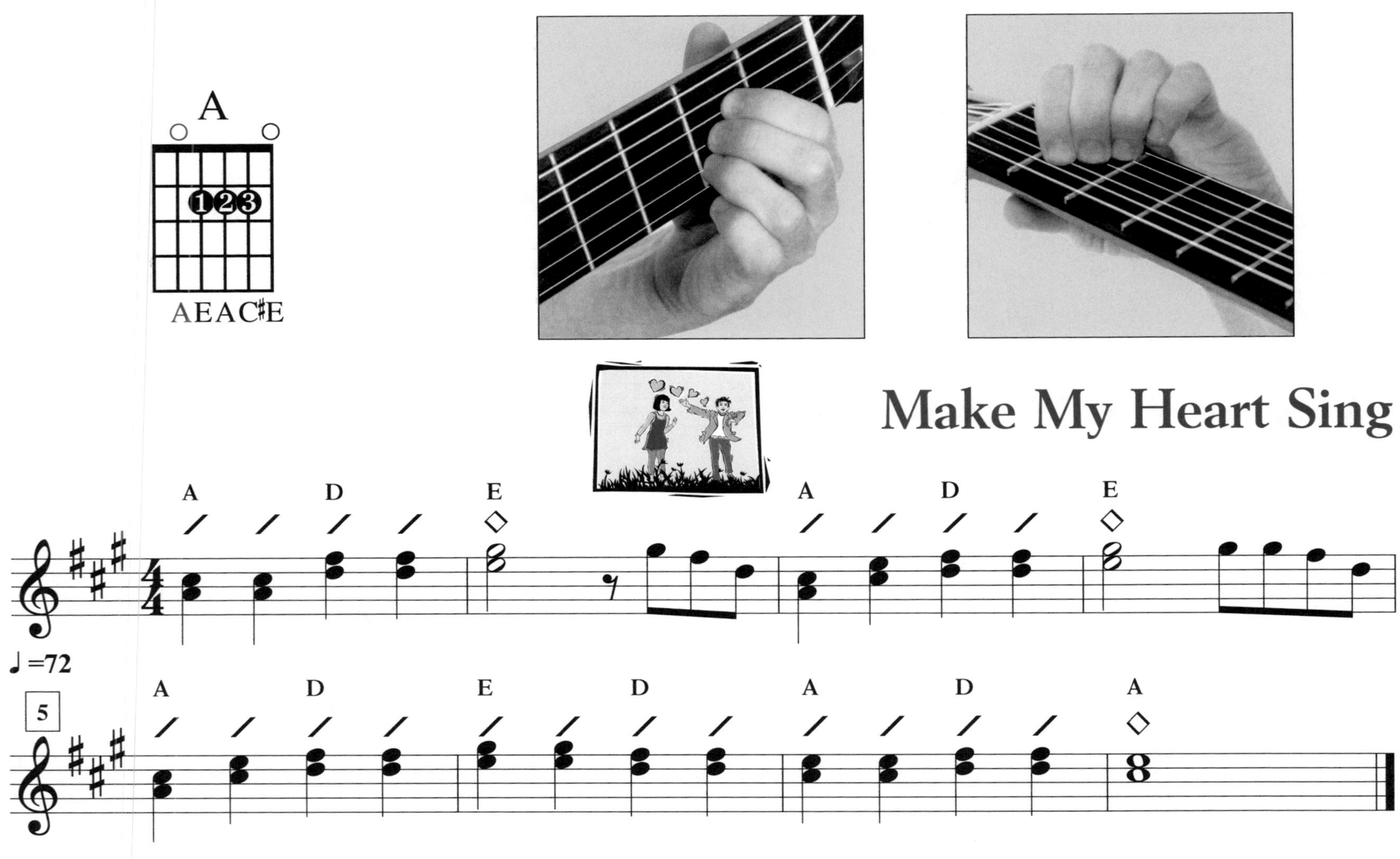

Here are two alternate fingerings for the A chord. There are no "right" or "wrong" fingerings for chords. Choose a fingering that allows you to use common and guide fingers whenever possible.

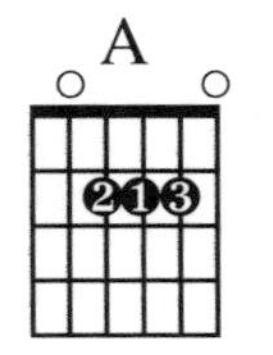

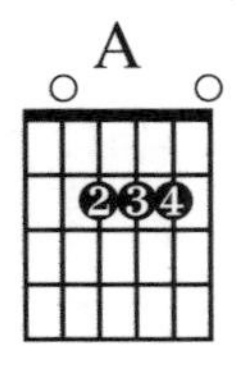

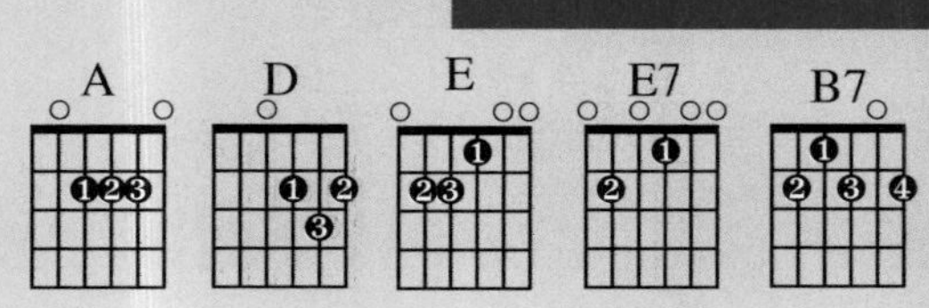

THE E SEVEN CHORD (E7)

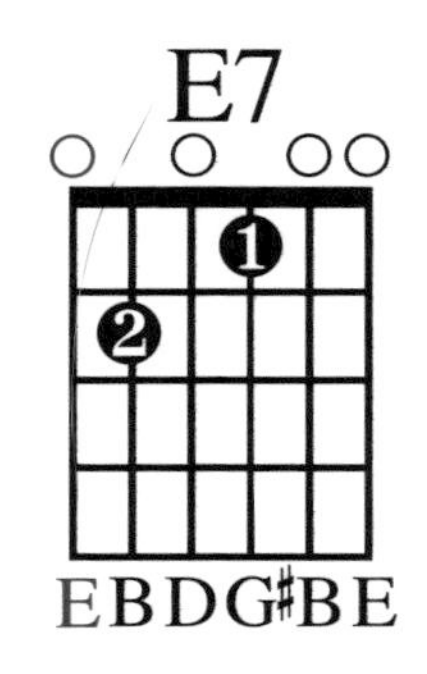

Rock-a-Bye Baby

Effie I. Crockett
(1857–1940)

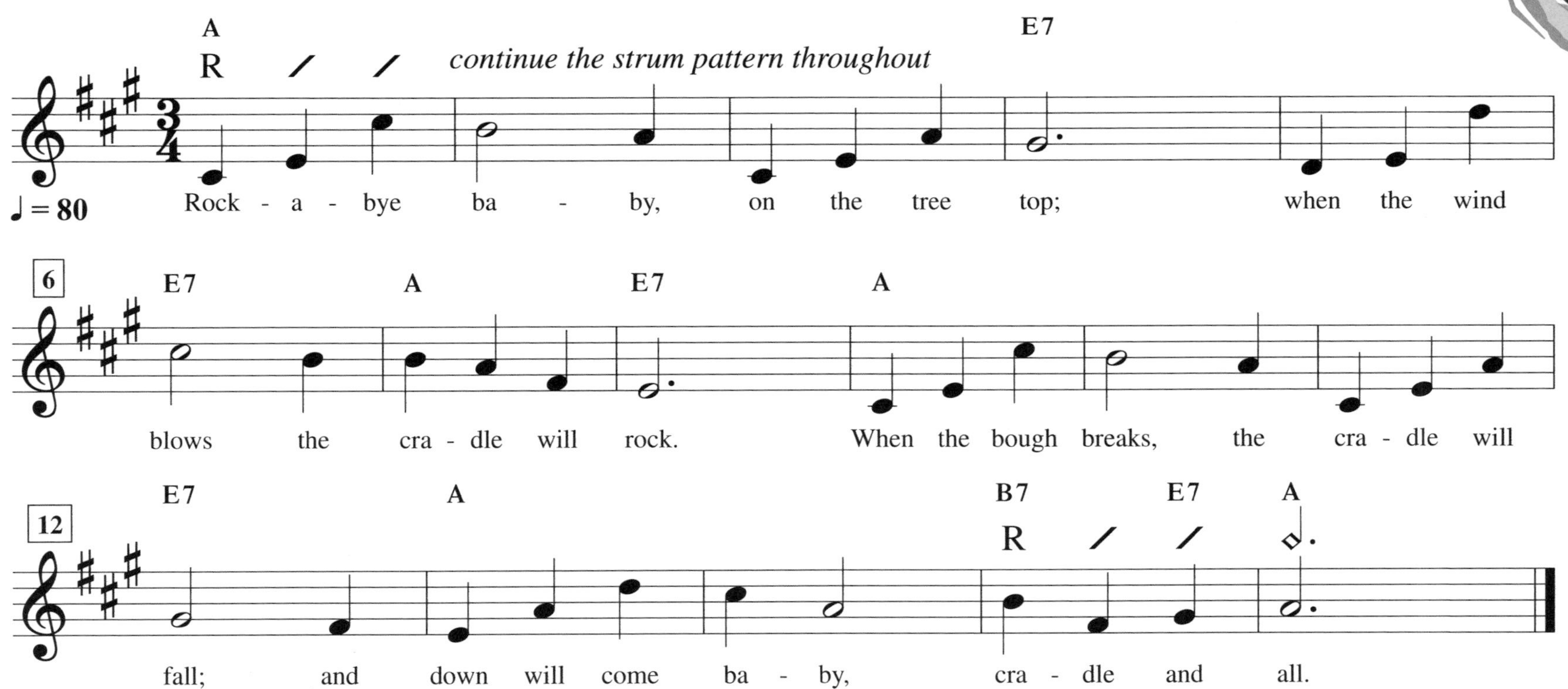

EIGHTH NOTE STRUMS

- A quarter note strum may be divided into two equal parts called **eighth note strums**.
- A single eighth note strum has a flag (♪). Two or more eighth notes may be connected by a beam (♫).

♪ = 1/2 beat ♫ = 1 beat ♫♫ = 2 beats

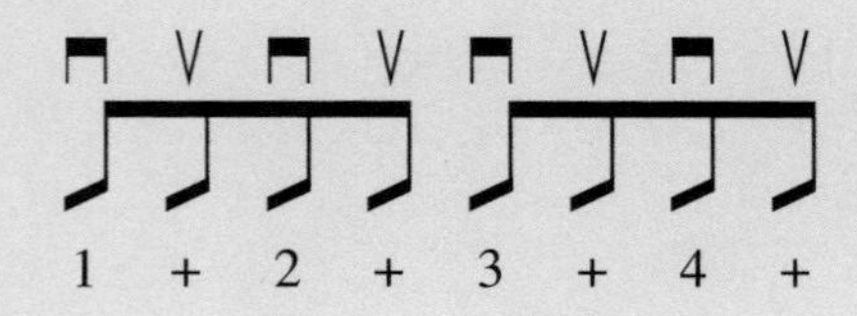

- Count aloud "***1** and **2** and **3** and **4** and*" several times evenly.
- Tap your foot down as you say each number.
  Lift your foot each time you say "*and.*"
- Now count "***1** and **2** and **3** and **4** and*" as you tap your foot down and up.
- Strum down (⊓) when you say each number, strum up (V) when you say "and."
  When playing an upstroke, you may strum three strings or less.

  You are now strumming the following eighth note rhythm pattern:

1 + 2 + 3 + 4 +

Practice this exercise with Em, using a steady down/up strum.

Use Eighth Note Strums with the following chord progressions:

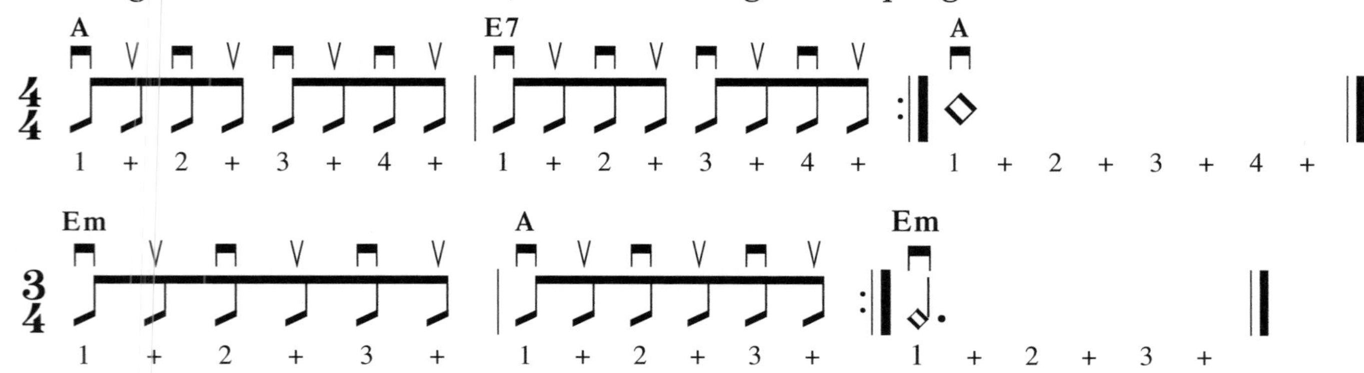

CHORD REVIEW CHART

A E7 Em D

The Sailor Song

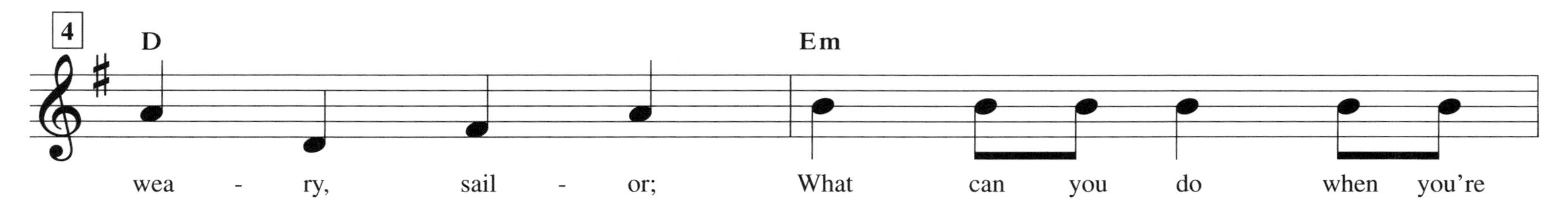

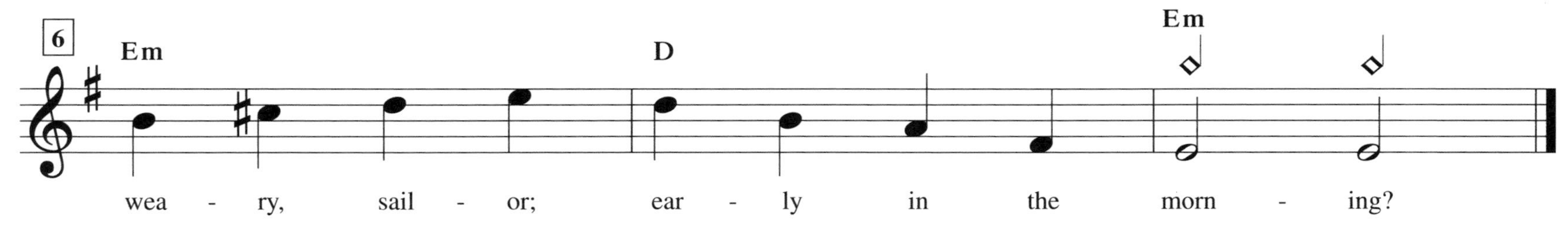

You may add an extra strum at the end of a song to create a stronger finish.

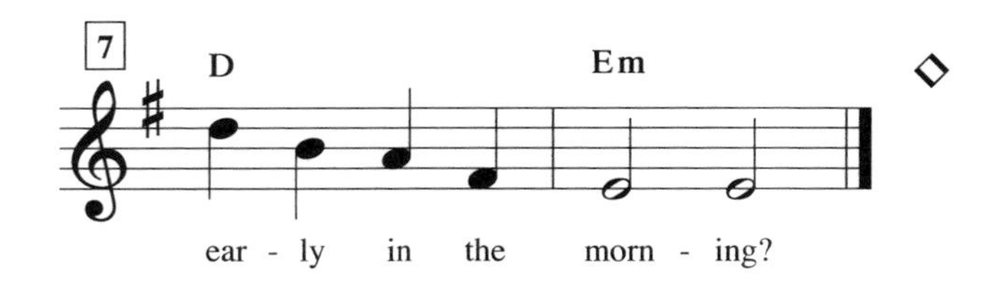

Play *Folias de España* on page 13 using the Eighth Note Strum in $\frac{3}{4}$ time as shown in the following example.

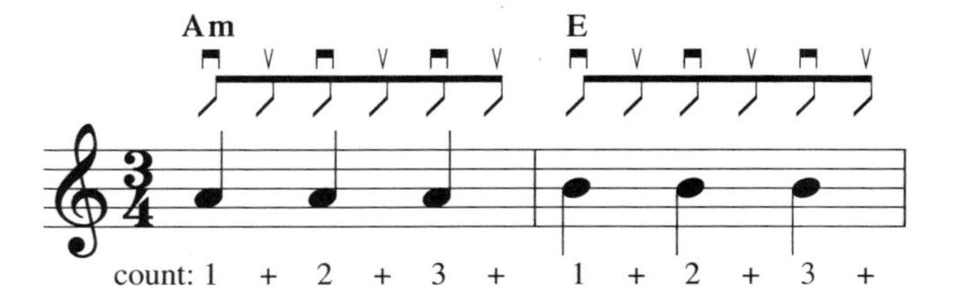

Red River Valley

American Folk Song
James J. Kerrigan

Listen carefully to your right-hand strum.
Keep your right hand moving very smoothly and evenly.

Playin' the Blues

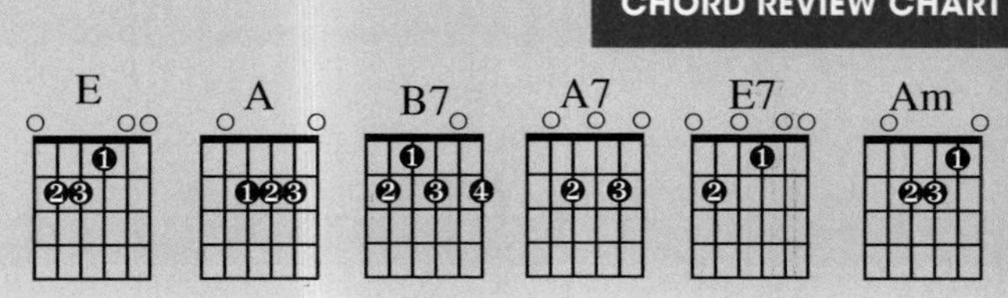

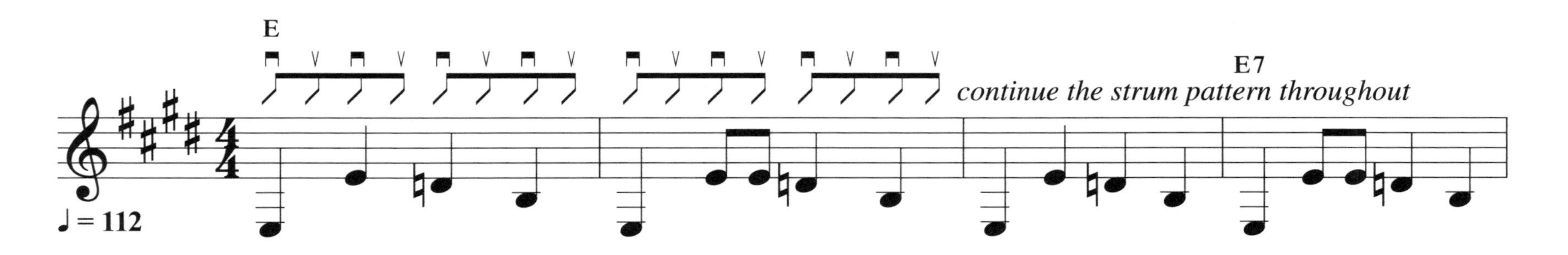

- Play slightly louder on beats one and three.
  Remember to play only two or three strings on the upstroke.
- Practice measure eleven separately.
  Always look ahead to the next chord.
  Play as slowly as necessary to keep a steady beat.

PUTTING IT ALL TOGETHER

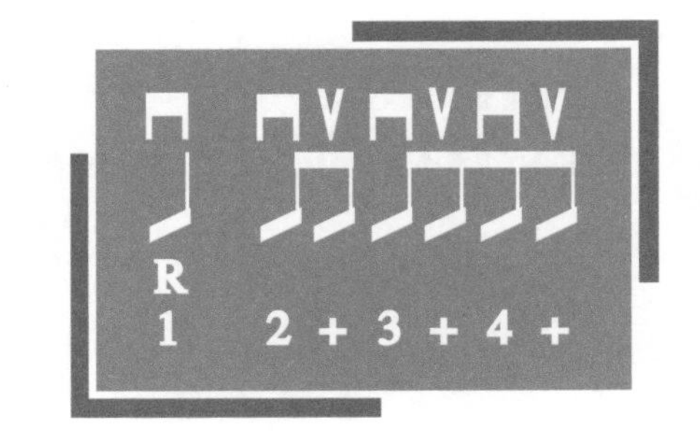

ROOT STRUM USING EIGHTH NOTES

- Play the root on beat one, and then strum eighth notes beginning on beat two.
- When playing upstrokes (V), strum three strings or less (not all six!).

Play the following two examples, using open-string roots.

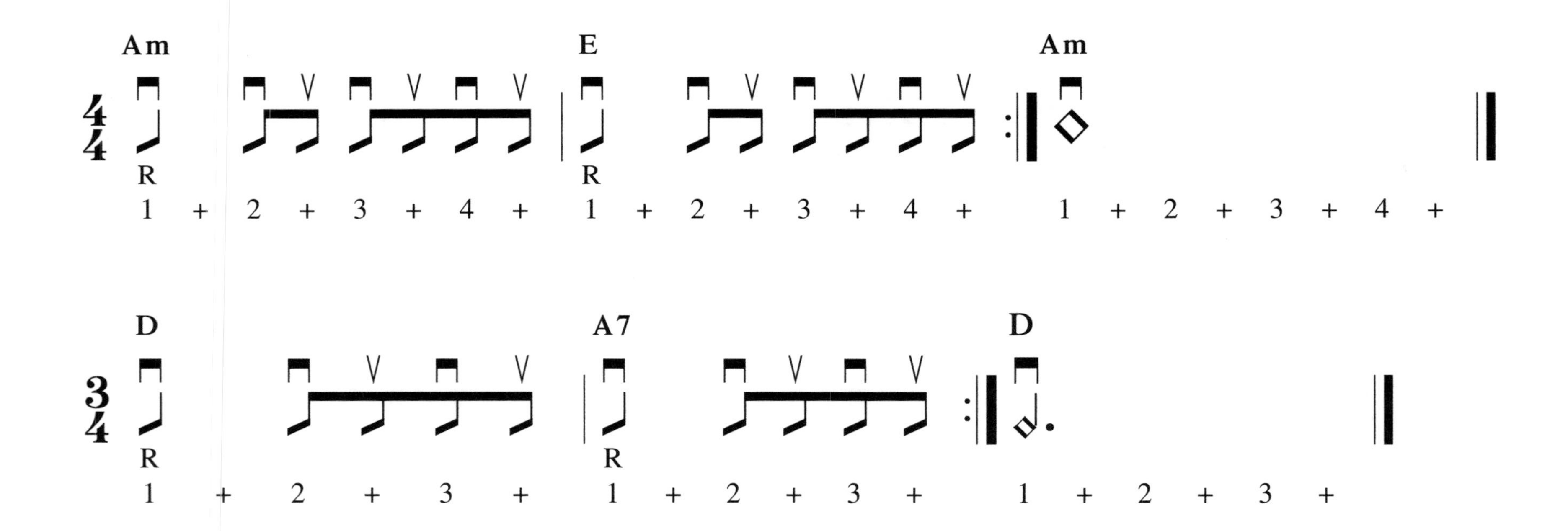

Use the above Root Strum patterns to play *It Ain't Gonna Rain No More* on page 14 and *She Played Her Guitar* on page 15.
The root notes will not be open strings.

CHORD REVIEW CHART

Am E D A7 C

G7 G D7 B7

I've Been Working on the Railroad

American Folk Song
Words by John Lang Sinclair (1880-1947)

Play *The Sailor Song* on page 23 with the Root Strum Using Eighth Notes.

24

Two Traditional Folk Songs

- If necessary, use the Chord Review Chart on page 31.
- You may want to try out various strum patterns for the following songs.

The House of the Rising Sun

American Folk Song

G

Aura Lee

Music by George R. Poulton (1828–1867)
Words by William Whiteman Fosdick (1825–1862)

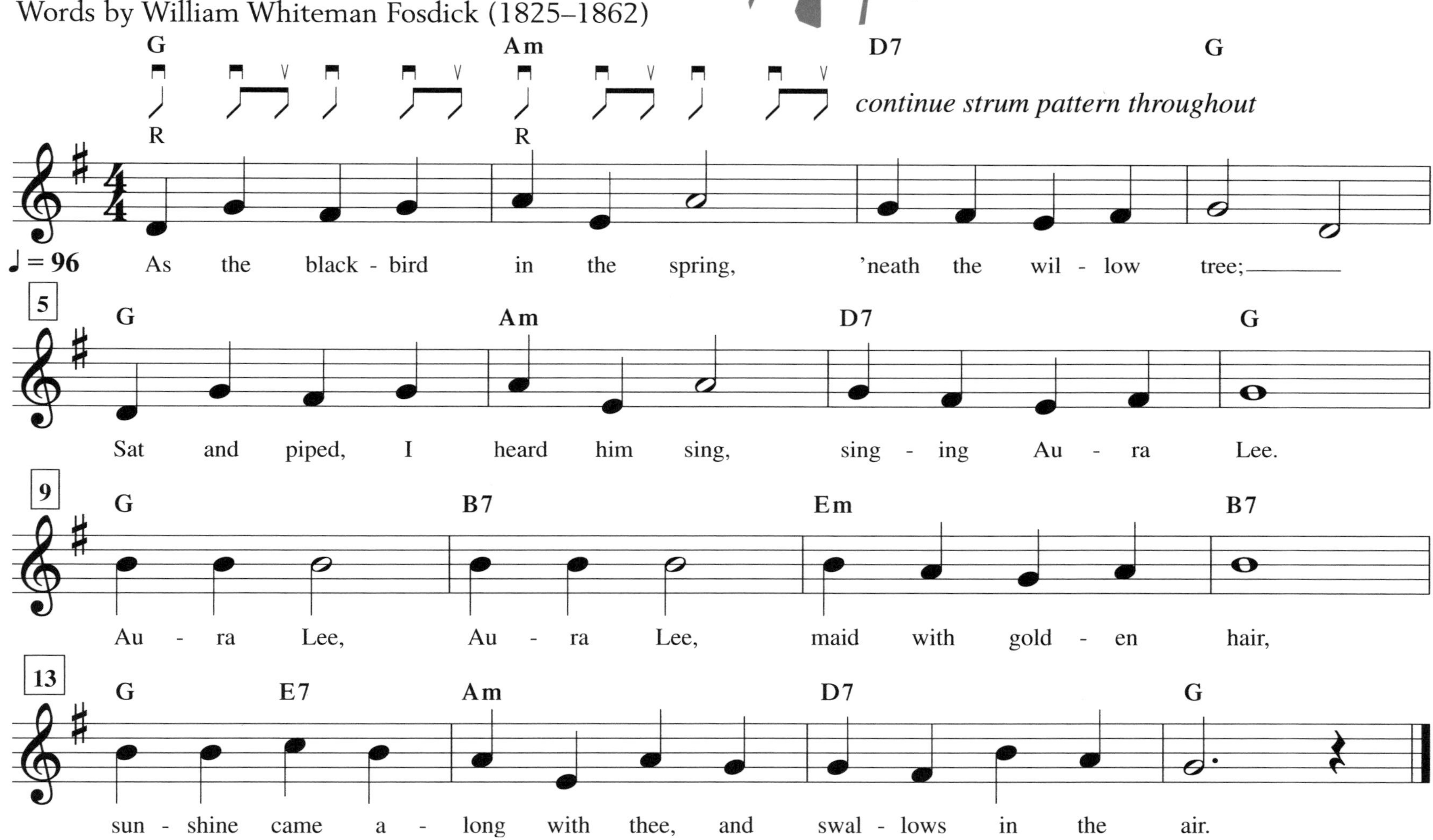

The suggested strum for *Aura Lee* is a variation of the Root Strum Using Eighth Notes on page 26.

Elvis Presley used the melody from *Aura Lee* in his hit song *Love Me Tender*.

CHORD REWARD

Playing With Shapes

Olympic Gold

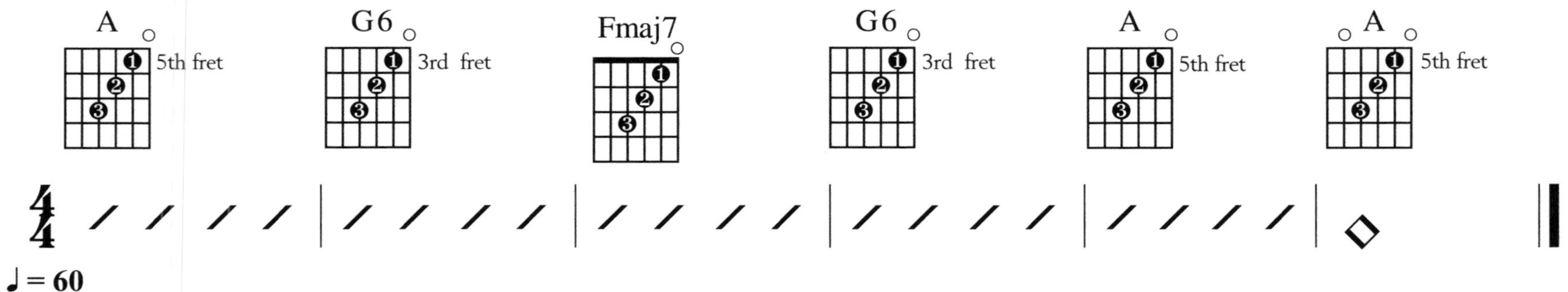

The Barre Chord

A *barre* chord (pronounced "bar") has one left-hand finger pressing down two or more strings at the same time.
Keeping your first finger just behind the fret will make it easier to get a good sound.
Practice the first chord in *Barre Chord Blues* until all three strings sound clear.

Barre Chord Blues

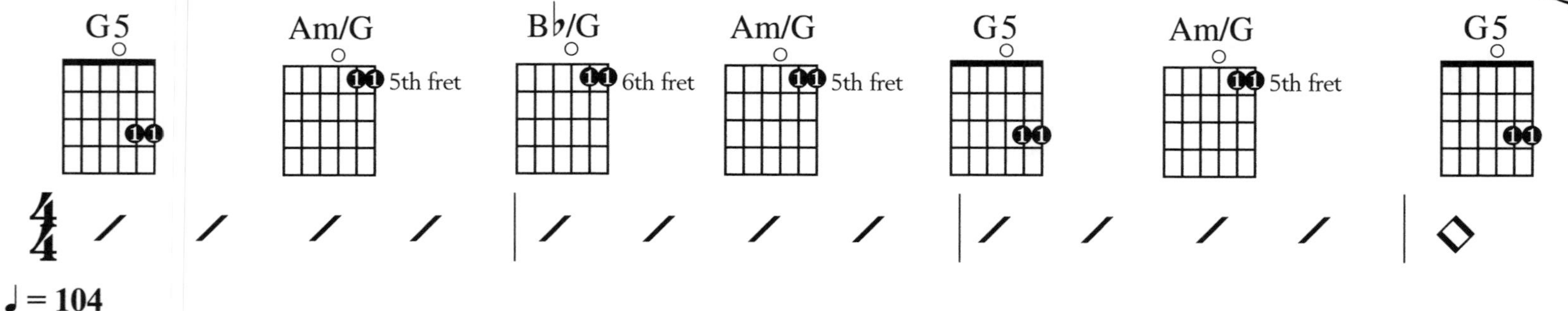

Experiment playing this chord on other frets as well.

CHORD REVIEW

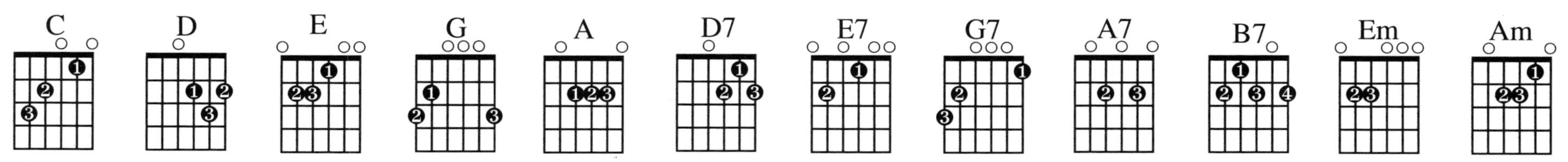

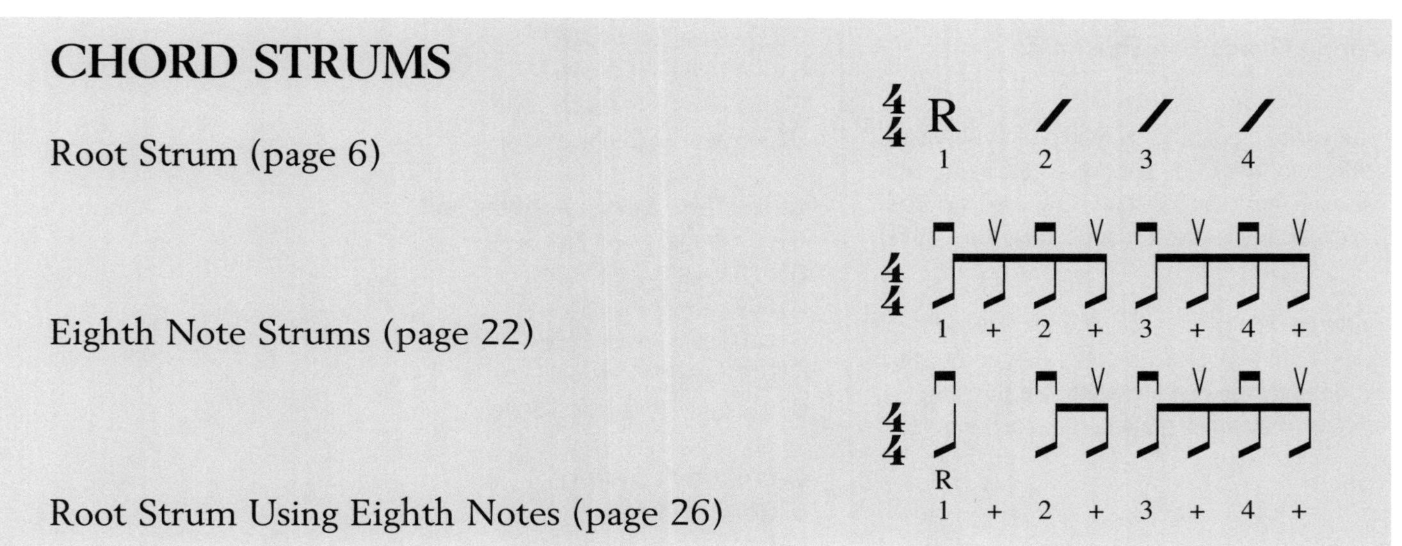

GLOSSARY

SIGN	TERM	DEFINITION
	common finger	A finger that remains in place when changing from one chord to another.
⊓	**downstroke**	The right hand strums the strings with a downward motion.
	guide finger	A finger that remains on a string while moving from one chord to another.
𝄽	**quarter rest**	A moment of silence for one beat.
	rhythm	Strum marks (♫ / 𝅗𝅥 𝅝) tell how long to hold each chord.
R	**root note**	The letter name of the chord.
V	**upstroke**	The right hand strums the strings with a upward motion.
	barre chord	A type of chord that has one left-hand finger playing two or more strings.

The FJH Young Beginner Guitar Method and Supplemental Material

The FJH Young Beginner Guitar Method is a well-conceived, graded guitar method designed especially for the younger beginner. Presenting one concept at a time, the method engages students with lively songs instead of exercises. Both teacher and student will enjoy the music right from the beginning! Adaptable in pick style or classical technique.

There are five publications in each of the three levels:
Lesson, Theory-Activity, Performance, Exploring Chords, and Christmas.

Level 1
Includes a pre-reading section that allows the student to play songs by reading fret numbers only. Natural notes in first position on strings one, two, and three are presented, along with basic rhythms. Dynamics are also introduced to develop musicianship at an early level. Includes optional teacher duets with chord names. Rhythmic accuracy is stressed throughout the method.

Level 2
Chords are introduced along with the natural notes on strings four, five, and six. New concepts include eighth notes, chromatics (sharps, flats and naturals), pick-up notes, ties, and rests. Students are encouraged to strum chords to accompany the melody whenever possible. Many optional teacher duets are included. (Students may enjoy playing the teacher duet parts as well!)

Level 3
In Lesson Book 3 the students learn complete chords with many opportunities to strum while the teacher plays the melody. New concepts include: dotted quarter notes, hammer-ons and pull-offs, major and minor pentatonic scales, major key theory and major scales, power chords, palm mute, solo styles, and music in Second Position. Music styles include popular, rock 'n' roll, blues, classics, multi-cultural, and music from various eras.

After the completion of Young Beginner Level 3 students move into **Everybody's Guitar Method**: **G1025 Book 1** if a review is needed; **G1030 Book 2** is the usual choice; **G1048** combines both Books 1 and 2 using tablature.

G1025

G1030

G1048

Supplemental Material for The FJH Young Beginner Guitar Method

GuitarTime Series Christmas
G1001 Primer Level Pick Style
G1002 Level 1 Pick Style
G1003 Level 2 Pick Style
G1004 Level 3 Pick Style
G1005 Level 1 Classical Style
G1006 Level 2 Classical Style

GuitarTime Series Popular Folk
G1007 Primer Level Pick Style
G1008 Level 1 Pick Style
G1009 Level 2 Pick Style
G1010 Level 3 Pick Style
G1011 Level 1 Classical Style
G1012 Level 2 Classical Style

Everybody's Series
G1026 Flash Cards
G1029 Basic Guitar Chords
G1032 Basic Guitar Scales
G1042 Strum & Play Guitar Chords
G1043 Guitar Ensembles
G1049 Ukulele Method 1
G1062 Electric Bass Method 1

Other Publications
G1058 My First Easy To Play Guitar TAB Book
G1060 My First Easy To Play Guitar Scale Book
G1061 My First Easy To Play Guitar Chord Book
G1059 The Big & Easy Songbook for Guitar with Tablature
G1054 The Big & Easy Christmas Songbook for Guitar with Tablature
G1055 The Big & Easy Songbook for Ukulele with Tablature
G1074 The Big & Easy Christmas Songbook for Ukulele with Tablature